Area

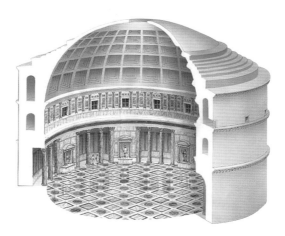

BLACKBIRCH PRESS

An imprint of Thomson Gale, a part of The Thomson Corporation

THOMSON

GALE

Detroit • New York • San Francisco • San Diego • New Haven, Conn. • Waterville, Maine • London • Munich

THOMSON

GALE

Consultant: Kimi Hosoume
Associate Director of GEMS (Great
   Explorations in Math and Science),
Director of PEACHES (Primary
   Explorations for Adults, Children,
   and Educators in Science),
Lawrence Hall of Science,
University of California,
Berkeley, California

For The Brown Reference Group plc
Text: Chris Woodford
Project Editor: Lesley Campbell-Wright
Designer: Lynne Ross
Picture Researcher: Susy Forbes
Illustrator: Darren Awuah
Managing Editor: Bridget Giles
Children's Publisher: Anne O'Daly
Production Director: Alastair Gourlay
Editorial Director: Lindsey Lowe

PHOTOGRAPHIC CREDITS
The Brown Reference Group plc: Edward Allwright 19, 28, 29; **Corbis:** Alan Schein
Photography 9, Rodney Hyett/Elizabeth Whiting & Associates 16, London Aerial Photo
Library 23, Jose Luis Pelaez, Inc. 22; **NASA:** 13, 20, 25, 26, 27t&b; **Photos.com:** 6, 12, 14.

Front cover: **The Brown Reference Group plc:** Edward Allwright

LIBRARY OF CONGRESS CATALOGING-IN-PUBLICATION DATA

Woodford, Chris.
 Area / by Chris Woodford.
   p. cm. — (How do we measure?)
 Includes bibliographical references and index.
  ISBN 1-4103-0366-7 (hard cover : alk. paper) — ISBN 1-4103-0522-8 (pbk. : alk.
paper)
  1. Area measurement—Juvenile literature. I. Title II. Series: Woodford, Chris.
How do we measure?

 QA465.W65 2005
 516.2—dc22

                                         2004018674

Contents

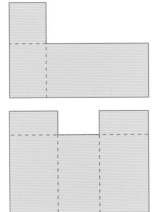

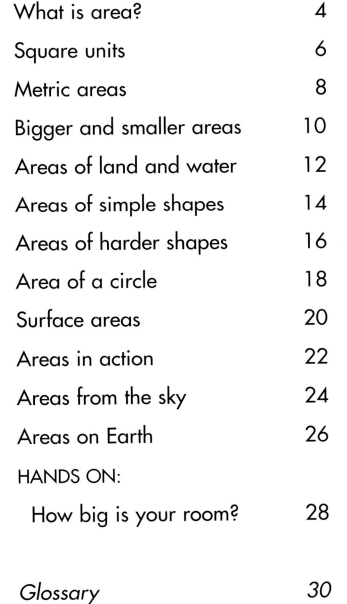

What is area?

Suppose you wanted to paint the walls of your room. You could figure out how many cans of paint to buy if you know how big the walls are. The size of a flat surface, such as a wall, is called its area. A big wall has a larger area than a small wall.

To figure out the area of a wall, you need to know both its length and its height. The length is the distance across the wall.

The height of a wall is the distance from the floor to the ceiling. The length of a wall is the distance across the wall from one corner of the room to another. The area of the wall is its length multiplied by its height.

area = length x height

length

height

Length, area, and perimeter

A rectangle is a shape with four sides and four right angles. We can find the length of a rectangular field by measuring it in one direction. The area of the field is its length times its width. The perimeter of the field is the distance around the area. That is the length of all the edges added together.

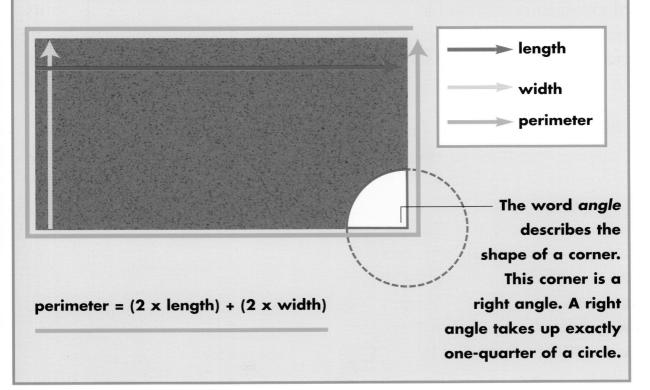

length

width

perimeter

perimeter = (2 x length) + (2 x width)

The word *angle* describes the shape of a corner. This corner is a right angle. A right angle takes up exactly one-quarter of a circle.

The height is the distance from floor to ceiling. The area of a wall is the length times the height. If the wall were longer or higher, it would have more area.

Being able to measure area is very useful at home, at school, and at work. Measuring area is also useful in geography, which is the study of our planet, Earth. Area helps us find out more about Earth's surface and how it is changing.

Square units

We measure lengths and distances with units such as inches, feet, and yards. Areas are measured in a different way. They have their own measurements called square units.

Measuring floor area

Suppose the floor of a room is covered in square tiles. Each tile is a foot wide and a foot long. We could say the area of each tile measures 1 foot by 1 foot. There is a shorter way of saying that. We can say the area is 1 square foot. A square foot is a measurement of area.

Suppose the whole floor is five tiles wide and four tiles long. The total area of the floor must be five times four, or 20 squares. Since each tile is 1 square foot, the area of the room is 20 square feet.

This is 1 square inch.

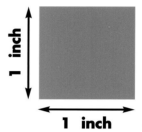

1 inch (height)
1 inch (width)

Compare it to a postage stamp:

1 square foot = 12 x 12 inches
            = 144 square inches

1 square yard = 3 x 3 feet
            = 9 square feet

1 square mile
    = 1,760 yards x 1,760 yards
    = 3,097,600 square yards

How length changes area

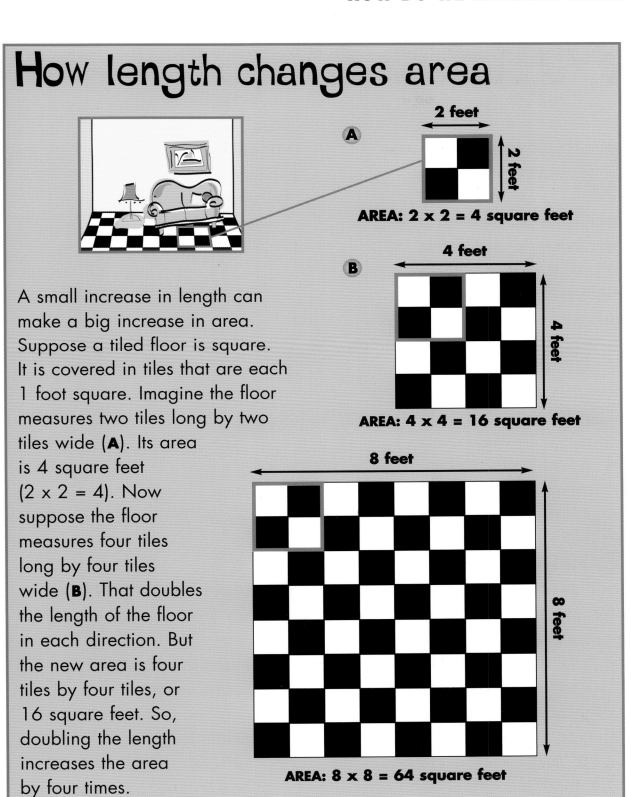

2 feet

A

2 feet

AREA: 2 x 2 = 4 square feet

4 feet

B

4 feet

AREA: 4 x 4 = 16 square feet

8 feet

8 feet

AREA: 8 x 8 = 64 square feet

A small increase in length can make a big increase in area. Suppose a tiled floor is square. It is covered in tiles that are each 1 foot square. Imagine the floor measures two tiles long by two tiles wide (**A**). Its area is 4 square feet (2 x 2 = 4). Now suppose the floor measures four tiles long by four tiles wide (**B**). That doubles the length of the floor in each direction. But the new area is four tiles by four tiles, or 16 square feet. So, doubling the length increases the area by four times.

Metric areas

Just as we can use metric units, such as centimeters and meters, to measure length, we can also use metric units to measure area. Metric areas include square millimeters, square centimeters, square meters, and square kilometers.

This blue square is 1 square centimeter. It holds 100 square millimeters.
- 1 square meter is the same as 10,000 square centimeters.
- 1 square kilometer is the same as 1 million square meters.

Metric and imperial

It is possible to change imperial measurements of area to metric measurements of area.

Metric measurements of area can also be changed back into imperial measurements of area.

IMPERIAL
1 square inch =
  6 ½ square centimeters
1 square foot =
  930 square centimeters
1 square yard =
  ⅘ square meter
1 square mile =
  2 ⅗ square kilometers

METRIC
1 square centimeter =
  ⅙ square inch
1 square meter =
  10 ¾ square feet
1 square meter =
  1 ⅕ square yards
1 square kilometer =
  ⅖ square miles

Square millimeters measure small things. You could use square centimeters to measure the area of a page in your reading book, for example.

Square meters could be used to measure the area of your school playground. People would use square kilometers to measure the area of a state or a country.

Square kilometers would be used to measure the area of the whole city.

Square meters would be used to measure the area of a baseball field.

Bigger and smaller areas

Square feet and square meters are good for measuring the areas of floors. Smaller areas than that can be measured in square inches or square centimeters.

Area of Mississippi
= 47,695 square miles
= 123,530 square kilometers

Mississippi

UNITED STATES

Area of United States
= 3,679,192 square miles
= 9,529,063 square kilometers

Comparing areas

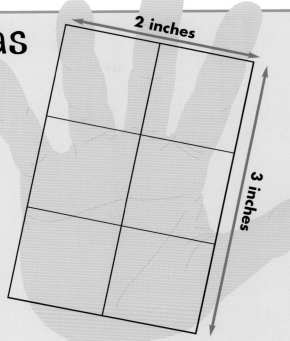

2 inches

3 inches

**Area of this hand
= 6 square inches
= 39 square centimeters**

Area of a typical library book's
cover = 100 square inches =
645 square centimeters

Area of a small room = 150
square feet = 14 square meters

Area of a football field = 57,600
square feet = 5,351 square meters

Area of a large field
= 1 million square feet
= 93,000 square meters

Area of the smallest U.S. state,
Rhode Island = 1,212 square
miles = 3,139 square kilometers

Area of the largest U.S. state,
Alaska = 591,004 square miles
= 1,530,700 square kilometers

Area of the United States
= 3,679,192 square miles
= 9,529,063 square kilometers

Area of Earth's surface = 200
million square miles = 510 million
square kilometers

Larger areas can be measured
in square yards or square miles
in the imperial system, or in
square meters or square

kilometers in the metric system.
A square mile measures one
mile long by one mile wide,
so it is a huge area.

Areas of land and water

Farmers and other people usually have to measure big areas of land. Land is measured in large units called acres. An acre measures 43,560 square feet. It is about three-fourths the size of a football field. The area of a farmer's field could be as much as 30 to 100 acres. In the metric system, land is measured in hectares. A hectare is about 2.5 acres.

Farmers have to measure the area of their fields to figure out how much of a crop to plant.

We can measure very large areas of land in square miles. A square mile measures 1 mile long by 1 mile wide. It is the same size as 640 acres. A square mile is almost as big as 500 football fields!

The Great Lakes

Acres can be used to measure water as well as land. The biggest areas of water in North America are the Great Lakes. Each lake covers a huge area that is the same size as millions of football fields!

LAKE	AREA (square miles)	HOW MANY FOOTBALL FIELDS IS THAT?
1 Superior	31,700	15 million
2 Huron	23,000	11 million
3 Michigan	22,300	11 million
4 Erie	9,910	5 million
5 Ontario	7,550	4 million

Areas of simple shapes

It is easy to figure out the area of a square. A square is a kind of rectangle. A square has four sides of equal length and four right angles. For any rectangle, the area is simply the length times the width.

A rectangle is also a kind of parallelogram. A parallelogram is a shape whose sides are parallel.

length

height

Above is a parallelogram. The area of a parallelogram is its length times its height.

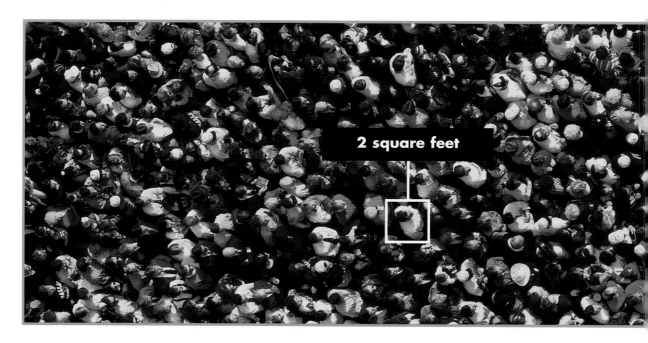

2 square feet

(Parallel lines are the same distance apart along their whole length.) A parellelogram's area is its length times its height.

It is also easy to figure out the area of a triangle. If you take two identical triangles and put them together, you make a parallelogram.

The area of each triangle is half the area of the parallelogram. The area of a parallelogram is its length times its height. The area of each triangle is equal to half of the parallelogram's area. So, the area of a triangle is half the length of its base times its height.

Two matching triangles put together make a parallelogram.

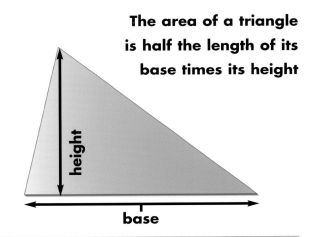

The area of a triangle is half the length of its base times its height

height

base

How many people in a crowd?

Huge crowds gather for rock concerts and other special events. People can figure out the size of a crowd if they know how big an area the crowd fills. Say each person takes up roughly 2 square feet of ground, and the total area of the place is 40,000 square feet. Dividing the total area of the place by the area each person takes up tells how many people are in the crowd. In this case, 40,000 divided by 2 is 20,000 people.

Areas of harder shapes

We often need to find the size of areas that are not simple shapes. Some oddly shaped areas look very hard to measure. But we can always take a complicated shape and divide it into simpler shapes. We can figure out the area of all the simple shapes.

Not all rooms are simple rectangles or squares.

What shapes can you find?

Choose an unusually shaped room in your house and draw its outline, or perimeter, on a piece of paper. Can you divide its shape into simpler shapes? In how many different ways can you divide the shape of the room?

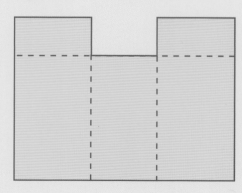

This picture shows the Pantheon. It was built in Rome, Italy, hundreds of years ago. People can estimate the area of the Pantheon using its floor tiles. An estimate is a good guess. You could measure the area of one tile, then count all the floor tiles. The total area is the area of one tile multiplied by the number of tiles. The actual area of the Pantheon is 12,625 square feet (1,173 square meters).

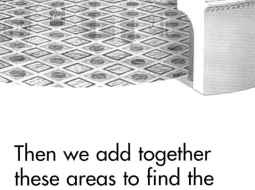

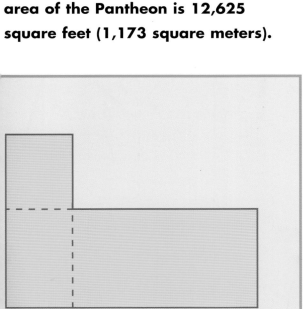

Then we add together these areas to find the area of the odd shape.

Suppose, for instance, that you needed to figure out the area of an L-shaped room in your house. You could split the L shape into three rectangles. The area of each rectangle is its length times its width. The area of the L-shaped room is the area of the three rectangles added together.

Area of a circle

A circle has no straight edges we can easily measure. So its area is harder to find than the area of a square. Even so, we can estimate the area of a circle easily.

Estimating means figuring something out roughly. An estimate is not exact but is close to the real figure.

Suppose you wanted to measure a circle's area. Draw a straight line from the center of the circle to the edge.

3 x r x r = area of a circle

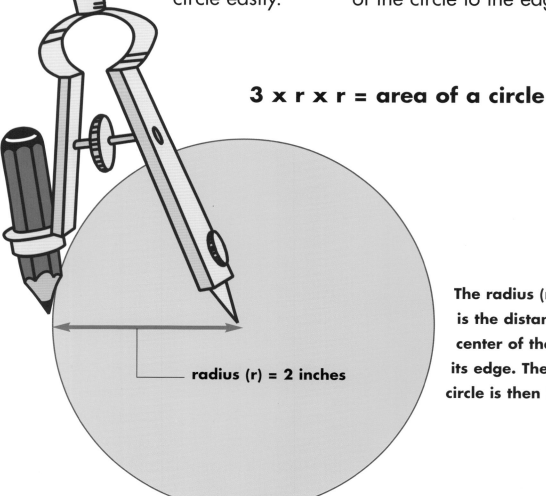

radius (r) = 2 inches

The radius (r) of a circle is the distance from the center of the circle to its edge. The area of the circle is then 3 x r x r.

The magic number pi

To get the exact area of a circle, we use a special number called pi. This number is often written like this: π. Pi is the number 3.141. To figure out the exact area of a circle, do this:

3.141 x r x r = area

You will need to use a calculator!

Once you have figured out the radius of the circle, you can find out the circle's exact area using 3.141 x r x r.

That length is called the radius (r). If you know a circle's radius, you can estimate the circle's area by doing this:

3 x r x r

If you swap "r" for your circle's radius, the answer is the area of your circle. Imagine that the radius of your circle is 2 inches. Can you figure out the area? (The area is 3 x 2 x 2 = 12 square inches.)

Surface areas

It is not only flat things that have an area. A tennis ball is a curved object called a sphere. The part of the sphere we can see is its outer surface. That surface has an area. We call it the surface area.

The surface area of a tennis ball is about 25 square inches (160 square centimeters).

A photograph of Earth taken from space. Earth's surface area is about 200 million square miles (510 million square kilometers).

Surface of a cube

How can we find the surface area of a cube? A cube has six identical faces. Each of these faces is a square. The area of a square is the length of one side times itself, or its height times its width. So the surface area of a cube must be six times bigger.

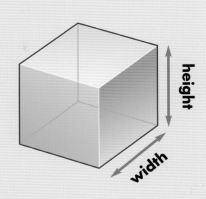

If we flatten out a cube, we can see that it is made up of six identical faces. Each face is a square. So the area of the cube is 6 x height x width.

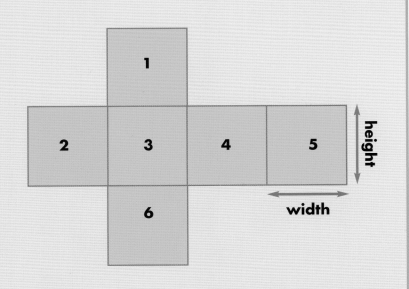

Our planet, Earth, is a bit like a gigantic tennis ball. We do not notice that Earth is round because it is so big, unless we see photographs of Earth taken from space. Some parts of Earth are covered by fields, tennis courts, and swimming pools. To us, these things look like flat areas. In fact, they sit atop Earth's curved surface. Every field on Earth makes up a tiny part of its huge surface area.

Areas in action

A reas can be useful in everyday life. Farmers often need to know how much seed to plant in their fields. One way they can do this is to measure the area of each field. Then they know how much seed to buy and how much to plant so their crops grow evenly.

Areas around your home

Areas can be a big help at home. They can help you figure out how much icing to put on a birthday cake. If you are wrapping a present, you must know how much paper you need before you start. If you know the size, or area, of the present, that tells you how much wrapping paper you need. Understanding areas is also helpful for making clothes. If you make clothes from a pattern, you can figure out how much cloth you need.

You need more paper to wrap bigger presents.

Area is also very useful for builders. If people are planning a new highway, they need to know how much space it will take up.

By figuring out the area of land they need, they can find out how much material they

When people are building a new highway, they need to know how much space, or area, it will take up so they get enough materials.

need to build the road. They can also figure out how much the highway will cost to build.

Areas from the sky

Suppose people want to measure the area of a country. It is not an easy thing to do. First of all, a country is not a simple shape. It has lots of jagged bits around the edges. And even a small country takes up a huge area. It would be very hard to measure a country with a ruler!

Larger areas are best measured from the sky, using a photograph of the ground taken from high up in an airplane. This kind of photograph is called an aerial photograph.

On an aerial photograph, buildings, fields, and whole cities turn into squares and other simple shapes. If we measure their areas on the photograph with a ruler, we can figure out their real areas by scaling up.

Scaling up

Suppose we have an aerial photograph of a park that we know the area of. We might measure the area of the park on the photograph.

Suppose we find that it takes up 1 square inch on the photograph. In real life the park is 1 acre.

So we know that a square inch on the photograph is the same as 1 acre of real land.

Now suppose we measure a different park on the photograph and find it is 12 square inches. Its real size must be 12 times 1 acre, or 12 acres:

$$12 \times 1 = 12 \text{ acres.}$$

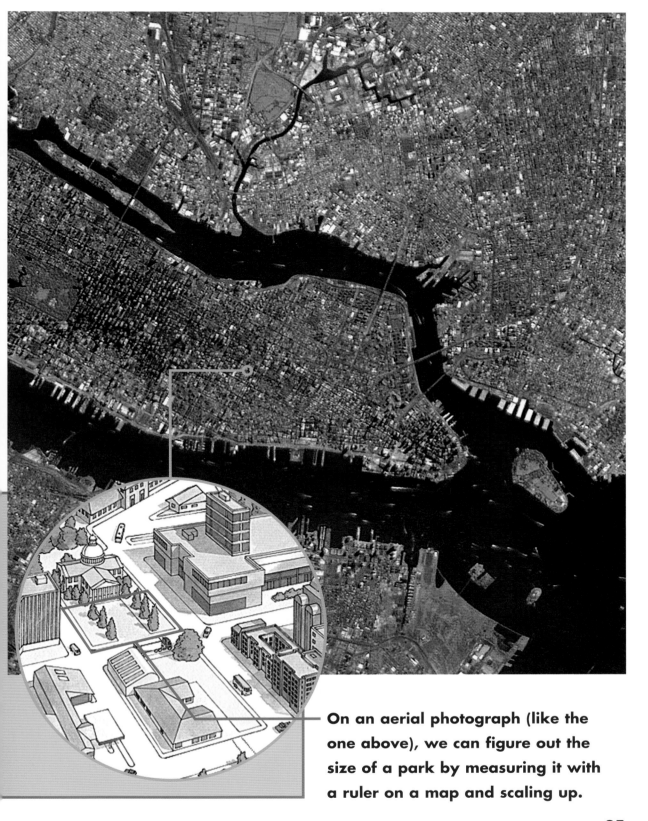

On an aerial photograph (like the one above), we can figure out the size of a park by measuring it with a ruler on a map and scaling up.

Areas on Earth

Photographs taken from space satellites tell us a great deal about planet Earth.

A satellite is a spacecraft without a crew that orbits (or moves around) Earth hundreds of miles above the ground.

The study of Earth is called geography. One of the things satellite photographs show is that seven-tenths of Earth is covered by water.

This satellite photograph shows how much of Earth is covered by water.

Vanishing forests

Satellite photographs have helped people see that Earth's forests are disappearing. People use satellite photographs to measure the area covered by forests each year. Each year, forested areas get smaller.

These two satellite pictures of an area in Bolivia, South America, show how much forest (dark red areas) has disappeared between 1975 to 2000. People have cut down forests to grow soybeans.

Satellite photographs also show us the areas of the continents. They help us measure the area of different states. They show how much of Earth's area is farmland and how much is covered by towns and cities.

If people take a satellite photograph from the same place every year, they can see how Earth is changing. Scientists are using satellite photographs to study global warming. That is the way Earth is slowly warming up because of things people do, such as burning coal and gas. Satellite photographs show the area of ice at the North Pole is slowly getting smaller. That suggests Earth is getting hotter. Studying areas is one way we can help save our planet.

How big is your room?

You will need:

- A large packet of paper (such as computer printer paper)
- A ruler
- A pencil

It is easy to estimate the size of your room. Here is how you can do it.

1 First measure the area of one piece of paper. Use the ruler to measure its length in inches. Then measure its width in inches.

Multiply the length of the paper by its width. Write down the result. That is the paper's area. If the length and width are both in inches, the area of the paper is in square inches. Write "square inches" after the number you wrote down.

2 Take some more paper out of the packet. Now very carefully cover the floor of your room with pieces of paper.

4 Multiply this number by the area of the first sheet of paper. The number you get is an estimate of the area of your floor in square inches.

Helpful hint

Make sure the edges of the paper touch. But do not let the papers cover each other. Try to cover the floor completely so that all you can see is paper. There will be parts of the floor that you cannot cover. Leave those areas.

Can you figure out other ways to measure the area of your room?

3 When the floor is covered as completely as possible, count how many pieces of paper you have put down.

Glossary

area The amount of space taken up by the surface of something.

diameter The distance across a circle from one edge to the other, through the center.

estimate A rough measurement.

geography The study of Earth.

length The distance between two points, usually measured in a straight line.

map A plan of some part of Earth. A map is drawn as though from high up looking down.

parallel Straight lines that are always the same distance apart.

parallelogram A four-sided shape in which every side is parallel to the opposite side.

perimeter The distance around the edge of a shape.

pi A number used to figure out areas of circles. Pi has the value 3.141 and is often written as the symbol π.

radius The distance from the center of a circle to the edge.

rectangle A four-sided shape with right-angled corners.

right angle The angle made by two lines meeting at 90 degrees, such as at the corner of a square.

satellite An uncrewed spacecraft that can take photographs of Earth.

scale up To figure out how big something is from a map.

square foot A unit of area that measures 1 foot long by 1 foot wide.

square inch A unit of area that measures 1 inch long by 1 inch wide.

square mile A unit of area that measures 1 mile long by 1 mile wide.

square unit A measurement of area. Square feet and square inches are examples of square units.

square yard A unit of area that measures 1 yard long by 1 yard wide.

urface area The area that covers
he surface of an object.

unit A measurement of something.
Examples of units are inches and yards.

find out more

Books

Carol Vorderman, *How Math Works.*
New York: Penguin, 1996.

Greg Tang and Harry Briggs,
Math for All Seasons. New York:
Scholastic, 2002.

Jerry Pallotta and Rob Bolster,
*Hershey's Milk Chocolate Weights
and Measures.* New York: Cartwheel
Books/Scholastic, 2003.

Tom Robinson, *The Everything Kids'
Science Experiments Book.* Avon,
Mass.: Adams Media, 2001.

Web sites

un Brain: Shape Surveyor Geometry Game
ee if you can measure area and
erimeter in this online game
ww.funbrain.com/poly/index.html

**king America's Measure:
un Activities for Kids**
ots of information about
he metric system
ww.nist.gov/public_affairs/
  kids/metric.htm

USGS TerraWeb for Kids
Information, games, and activities
about satellite maps
terraweb.wr.usgs.gov/TRS/
  kids/links.html

Yahooligans: Measurements and Units
A useful collection of websites
about measurement
yahooligans.yahoo.com/Science_and
  _Nature/Measurements_and_Units

Index